"Gram, what is in the big crack?"
Brad said.
"Is it a big fat bug?"

"Let's look at it," Gram said.
"It's a big fat brown crab!"

Brad said, "Brown is a funny color for a crab."
Gram grins at Brad as he sits and gets wet.

"Look, Brad," Gram said. "Many crabs are brown. Some crabs are also blue, green, and tan."

"I like big crabs a lot!" Brad said. "Let's grab a net and trap big wet crabs!"

Gram has a quick trick.
Grab the back of the crab.
Its claws can not grab back!

Where is the big crab?
"It can dig, dig, dig!" Gram said.

"We did not trick the big crab,"
Brad said.
"It tricked you and me!"